Prolog Pages:

Prolog Pages:

Donald Wellman

*aha*dada

b o o k s

tokyo / toronto

Prolog Pages:

Jesse Glass, General Editor
Layout and Design: Joe Zanghi, Printed Matter Press

editorial address:

Ahadada Books
3158 Bentworth Drive
Burlington, Ontario
Canada L7M-1M2

Meikai University
8 Akemi, Urayasu-shi
Chiba-ken, Japan 279-8550

First Edition
Printed and Bound in Canada

ISBN 978-0-9808873-8-9

Some of this work has appeared in the following publications:

- "Previously," "Ensaladas," and "Madrid" in _BlazeVOX: Post-avant Poetries and Fiction_ (2005).
- "Madre," "El Palo," "Málaga I," "Málaga II," "In the Archbishop's Palace," "7.31" and "After Prados" in _Fascicle_ 2 (Winter 2006).
- "Insomnia," "Final Shadow," and "On Earth" from Emilio Prados' _Jardín cerrado_ in _Fascicle_ 2 (Winter 2006).
- "Tangier," "Organic Form," "Men Who Sublimate," "Granada," "Capileira," "Bizcas," "The Cartuja of Granada" and a photograph, "Arabesques," in the on-line and print editions of the journal, _Arabesques Review_ (Chlef, Algeria), March 2006.
- "Public Arts," "Reforma," "Tepotzotlán," "Architectural note for the New Year" and "Gallery" in the on-line journal _There_ (Fall 2006).
- "Dioses de Oaxaca," "San Agustín," "White Room" and "Sacrament" in _Eratio: Postmodern Poetry_ 8 (Fall 2006).
- _Xcp: Streetnotes_, Winter 2006.

Part I: Prolog Pages

Horizons give perspective.
Here they have been abolished.

Previously

1

If something or someone with properties similar to those of a machine had been wanted,
  then the impossibility of truly sharing might have been circumvented;
  but, at the time, who dared ask?

So I fled to the opposite end of all earthly lands:

....

2

The young age of your heart, poet, is not a shore
that the sea charges with its ragged surf,
teeth of love that nibble the edges of the land,
roaring sweetly.

No. Esa luz que en el mundo
no es ceniza última.
luz que nunca se abate como polvo en los labios,
eres tú, poeta, cuya mano y no la luna
yo vi en los cielos una noche brillando.

A strong breast that lays itself upon the ocean
breathes like the immense celestial tide
and opens its outspread arms and beats them,
caressing the far limits of the earth.

Translation and quotation from "El Poeta" in *Sombra del Paraíso* by Vicente Aleixandre.
The coast here is Aleixandre's native Málaga.

Ensaladas

Asparagus salad in a savory vinaigrette (white as once so tender in youth,
awaiting reunion then, with one I loved).
      Now navigate the Plaza Mayor,
        its inviting tables and handsome waiters.
Murals of pink-skinned youth in leafy glades
        either side the shield of the municipal corporation.
The near view absorbs the eye
Cold cider from Asturias and a "revuelta con gulas."

My instruction until now
        has been "to dance sitting down."
        (a large brown bear in that image)
My baroque juxtapositions, assorted, folded
        laundry in a suitcase, phrases and images,
        furniture.

...because I have my notebook open, and so I am writing

Handsome is as handsome does in wig or frock coat,
18th century men enjoyed sexual privilege.
The bo-peeps showed their petticoats.

On the Plaza Santa Ana, three young people
ask to share my table.
The waiter shoos them off
Are they thieves, well-known to him?

In "Perspectivas Imperiales," Edward Said comments upon the arrogance of empire so palpable
in the foreign policy and military interventions of the United States in Palestine and Iraq.'
El Almanaque, 26 Julio 2003.

Requiescat, 25 September 2003.

To remain invisible among the beech trees and holm oaks appears the wisest course
[Machado's "negra encina campesina"].

At their leisure, did the philosophical men of 18th century France and Spain
dress in turban and pantaloons?
Who dares to call the gods our play things
as someone might make reference to statuettes
or bric-a-brac
and not acknowledge the opposite?
The gods do not impress us with their morality,
dismembering their offspring,
transforming mortals into beasts
in their lust for hybrid procreation;
they take pleasure in administering famine, death, old age,
indiscriminate in destruction.

As once in Havana, revealed itself
to have many hands with which to swat at flies,
but not the stomach of a god.

Requiescat 17 July 2003.

Celia Cruz, la Guarachera de Cuba.

...because he writes in his notebook

«This one here is a stranger whose eyes scan the room and in turn he writes without stopping. He can't be a spy because spies work with greater secrecy. He wants to walk, unperceived and alone He undertakes to denounce the stranger who sits in the shadows. He asks if it is the custom to serve the tea so hot. At the first sip he burned his tongue, gave a small cry and made a stupid face He could be a poet or writer. They told him that this 'café where merchants gather' is famous because the best poets of Baghdad meet here to read their compositions. He hopes that a place with this famous and creative ambience will inspire him. Why not? He must come from a cold country because he sweats so much and looks at the ceiling fan with desperation, yet without electricity the wheel doesn't turn. What things and in what language does he write in his little notebook. Surely his thoughts might be a good subject for the pronouncements and debate that will occur in the gathering here this afternoon.»

Mario Vargas Llosa, reporting from Baghdad for *El Pais Semanal*, 27 July 2003.

....

Eugène Delacroix,
Moroccan Notebook,
1832

Pages that participate
in a history of
notebook keeping.
Rough thoughts
become fixed; gauze
of enlightenment
constructs and evident
orientalisms map
vulnerabilities.

Madre

Leticia is not a friendly person,
speaks through her teeth,
not moving her lips.

Her lentil soup is fragrant
with coriander and cilantro.

I have tracked dust from my sandals
onto her newly washed floors.
I am unclean; I fail to understand
the combat that she shapes between us
in defiance of my undifferentiated powers.

In this I have become
responsible for her cruelties.

Her bocarones fried in a delicate batter.

Still I would not be her son or husband
who suffer for love.

El Palo

An atom of the pain of exile glints in the immigrant's yellow eyes.
The poetry of the unhoused experience is not glamorous.

Poets who attain a cosmopolitan panache
squint with the soreness of that rictus
in their hearts. For the uneducated, dispossessed
safety and poverty are kin obsessions.

The wind off the water is brisk;
at night the sheets tangle
            with sweating limbs and aching feet.
During night terrors, I am always only in my forties.

Lanterns bounce on wires, wind-tossed, paper torn.
Anonymous immigrants sweep the plaza,
a civic monument to the poet, Emilio Prados.

To admire the old men who sit dispassionately at dominos,
does it show how worn the garments of my spirit have become?
Africa, not far off, in the low lying haze.

"The Wind is in from Africa." Joni Mitchell wrote "Carey" while visiting Crete in 1970.

Málaga I

The clay dish rocks unevenly; it sits heavily.
The coffee too is superior at the Archbishop's Tavern.

Waves that crashed in the imagination
against the ramparts of the Alcazaba
no longer touch the palm-lined shore
with its most brilliant array of tropical flora,
Málaga's celebrated garden.

The new social spaces of apartment blocks
and municipal offices
fill the foreground
where Vandals embarked
for Roman Africa,
seamen who denied
that Jesus and God were one.

On a corner in that district, near the modern bullring,
in a house with a name like the cry of a hawk,
late into the early morning,
they sing the deep song,
"Casa Tiri"

Royally the banners and placards for
an exhibition of 19th century family photographs
drape the stanchion poles;
others display, biomorphic forms
of indeterminate connection to the coast.
Should I say more about my errors?

Susie asado
Bien asado

The Picasso Museum overlooks a Roman amphitheater.
Arab Andalucía persists in the white villages of the Sierra Nevada

A younger eye than mine imposes its register of indifference,
measured exuberance, on festival and department store,
the largest, El Corte Inglés, its corporate policies,
identified with fascism.

Málaga II

A woman of iron is a tyrant, her perfect intonation
"Cada madrugada"
Honeyed guitar and violin.
Inebriation beyond the pale of wine or dope
"Live the summer, feel the heat!"
On the Plaza de la Merced,
bodies move in unison, Nordic and Berber musicians.
Darbuka and sakara resonate,
fiery arpeggios on synthesizers.
Nightlong, the ganawa lacerate themselves,
        for the love of the camel-footed goddess,
        the flat of a knife repeatedly strikes the back of the neck.
Composite, rape and inexplicable tenderness.
Youth and inexplicable strength
The swagger and sway of the lord of the dance,
inexplicably baroque.

In the Archbishop's Palace
In a painting by Guillermo Perez Villalta,
Dos mujeres contemplando dos hombres, 1995,

Two men kiss, one shows greater passion than the other
who is being mounted, coiled within the legs
of the first. A screen of interlaced
ribbons, a trellis
through which two women watch
Greens and oranges suffused with a luminous yellow.

Boots that stand on their own, stiffened
with the heaviness of desire.

Flattened volumes elicit a response
very like viewing an engraving of a statue
in contrast to the experience of seeing form in the round.

The male is rational as painting requires, he writes,
the female instinctive with a talent for modeling.
Was he thinking of his mother's flour white hands?

He works space into allegories of resistance.
Does truth in design celebrate equally,
attraction and distaste for instinctive flesh?

Who is to explore the margin between the body, the sensorium, and some vague or hard and fast elsewhere? He drags the work of the imagination into the world: "no es real hasta que yo la invento, la traigo a este mundo, entonces sí que te puedes tropezar con ella."

Lucia Extebarria and Sonia Nuñez Puente infer a sadistic impulse in his remarks.

On this beach, the lovelies lie topless in the summer sun.
The more I read of Prados the more he interests me

Is the nakedness of women simply a pleasure for them?
I can imagine feeling captive
to my or anyone's gaze.

Do the lovelies even love to be lovely?
I don't care for my own reflection
I'd like to think that they do.

For all I know I am the only American on this coast
or continent. I float out with the strong current
and swim back to shore for exercise

After Prados

Where do the borders of my soul begin?

The file of skiffs
sets out with nets
for the evening catch.

Each hull a luminous pastel,
my body awash with fluorescent waves.

Does the wind abrupt on my entrails?
Where are the suburbs of the city
or is it the silky ocean
that is my body?

Olives

Tangier

Is there a human creature whom no none notices or greets
because he doesn't know
hand signals or body language?
Not in these crowded alleys.
Even one who assumes that he belongs to the category of untouchables
finds that citizens greet him cordially.

Necessarily, kindness in business afflicts this one deeply, even bitterly,
unlike those who expect to be served courteously.

If he makes a good deal for an expensive item
and carries it away, is that plunder or trade?

...

The salesmen in the rug gallery often touched me with their hands as though I were a pet to be soothed. We circled each other, whimpering, not barking. I escaped once but to do so I had to yield my claim to the most beautiful rug in the world, the red one with multiple birds of paradise in the swirling center. Remember reading Avicenna's *Recital of the Birds*! I felt guilty in my freedom, but turning from the embrace of the first man, I met another who promised that he could make my dreams come true. I had already purchased the plate with sage green trefoil arabesques. My new acquaintance assured me that we were now friends for life. I promised to visit his brothers in Newton and Brookline when I got home. Boda is the family name. Then our courting began again. He offered me the opportunity to acquire the most beautiful rug in the world from among all those that had been previously owned. These were very beautiful, he whispered, and less costly than those that had tempted me earlier. Between friends, as we had become with our assurances like kisses, it was impossible to resist the seduction.

I carried my carpet from the medina to the ferry, from the ferry to the airport, looking forward to my homecoming, unfolding the Rabat red in my wilderness home, not a coin in my pocket for coffee or cognac.

Brooms, Bread, and Chicken

Organic Form

Nylon sacks of a fine mesh, each filled with a milk of foam pellets, so that two are
        pendulous, one more engorged than the other and tied off at its base, the fabric now of a
        brown rose hue, as a stocking might appear when rolled (Ernesto Neto).

A bracelet on the right wrist, smoking, the other arm withered. Her pudendum shaved,
        a rash visible; her dignity compels admiration (Andreas Serrano).

Abstract washes over a lead base in a series called "Stabat Mater" (James Brown).

Is my mind, for reason of private compulsions, drawn to this maternal theme
        among all other possibilities or is the pattern deeply woven into the fabric of the
        exhibition?

Sewing needles lying close together like grass
Each with a length of silver thread
The canvas shimmers, brushed by a wind or soft hand
"Carta retenida." Hilo, óleo sobre lino y agujas de coser
(Elena del Rivero).

In the most prominent spaces of the gallery are organic shapes in spiraling but collapsing
        forms (Tony Cragg).

Men Who Sublimate

Forming a masculine narrative, within these spaces,
the artist paints a fable in which he is the boy
who accompanied Jason on his quest for the Golden Fleece.
(Guillermo Pérez Villalta)

The search for respite includes Ed Ruscha's Sunset Strip
and Dario Villalba's *Picadilly Rent Boy.*
Did I speak to the lack of glamour in homelessness?

On another day, because of the eccentricities
concerning when I feel welcome in my lodging,
I go to Nerja for a swim in the caves.

When I was a boy, I saw how the new buildings crowded the shore.
I found beauty in the rusting remains of the cement and crushed stone industries.

Cinema of Greenaway

Suitcases of fish, of perfumes in differently tinted bottles, of money, of garters and
      brassieres.

A visually compelling use of photomontages in Peter Greenaway's *Suitcases
      of Tulse Luper,* a derivative film, so most critics have said, homage to Duchamp. Little
      numbers like those on a schematics on some faces

      Was it a *Gunslinger* epic in that Moab of his imagination or a Dylan song that spoke to
      embarrassment and torture, American fascist tactics back in the days of law and order.
      The boy's genitals examined to verify racial purity, the agony of flesh, coated with hone
      and left to the insects and the blistering sun. Whose traumas are these, if not mine? An
      easy sadism!

Daphne

She is a Professor of massage therapies. Her parents were born in Bangladesh. Malnutrition has shaped her facial bones. When she asked my age, I told her the truth.

For all that, I have fallen in love with the Archbishop's daughter. After the obligatory tour of the Santa Iglesia Cathedral, with its gold altar to Saint Barbara and its porcelain Blessed Mary of Victoria, we had coffee. We hardly spoke. She is a sensitive and radiant person.

The segue is I have also seen the christening gown of Picasso and the photographs of the poet with his children at La Californie.

I have vowed to be a loving grandfather.

From the mud of origins, my clay pot,
wells with desire to be precise
in my skin, like that of a truly old man
when he attains the calm of a statue

I have had three periods of extended solitude in my life; this is the third,
Tres tiempos de soledad.
The clientele in the hotels is very British, some Danish
I often prefer to dine alone
and declaim anonymously of my vagabondage.

Can I go wrong on garden paths
that return to a fountain, El Generalife, whose watered and whispering stairs
are sacred to poets, some murdered, some dying in exile?

Granada

In what sense did I earn the privilege
     of sitting in the courtyard of the Fountain of the Four Lions?
To quench my thirst with waters from Lanjarón?
Or to write in this notebook, its cover incorporating Caneletto,
     his disconcerting 18th century gentlemen
admiring the campanile.
Advice, I have heard repeatedly, warns the traveler not to bathe in the lagoons of Venice.
At night, looking over the valley of the Daro toward the Alhambra
the view approximates my conception of heaven.
Looking up into the vaults of the Palacios Nazaríes, that vertigo returns.
Possibly in my childhood, a different castle on a different hill had a similar effect? Briar Rose?
As if I were constrained to ask what is next, but I have not found anyone to whom
I am willing to pose
the necessary questions.
In murderous dreams I am my mother
My body becomes hers again..

Marriages

On the plazas of the Alhambra brides pose as directed by photographers,
cream taffeta, the fabric of fashion.
Each, slender amid evening shadows,
slippers embroidered with sequins.
Was it in the 19th century that woman began to be observed as fragments of persons?
A production of Yerma will follow in the garden of the Generalife.
Dark lament and relentless pulse of the fountain that is flamenco.
Hems glide over pavement
White stones laid amid gray
to form compass flowers
Four petals to each circle,
each leaf seeded with pearls.
The markets of Andalucía,
constructed from interlaced arcades and alleys,
perspectives that shrink horizons
to the near hand, excepting
the imperial view from palaces and minarets.

La Cabra Mecánica

The band read from *The Tropic of Capricorn*
as it pursued its mechanical
processes, connecting voice with instrument, instrument with hand, with pulse. Eyes glinting, th
    lyric soul carrying suitcases for the mafia
Excursions to the lagoon.
Satyrs lost in baroque foliage.
Mascara that mimes Faustian duende.

Capileira

The wind blows sleet into the gorge
I taste here the first crusty bread of these travels.
Is it a custom among mountain people to bake so?

Then thunder as I relive the crawling on the cliff faces that haunt my voyage.

Below me the Moorish terracing continues to hold the gardens in their places on the slopes
Yellow wheat and olives with a tender, smoky hue.
What auguries?

The dark voice
and the madness in the feet of the chorus
What amplifications?
Cherries and currants that I associate with childhood.

She had been hiking in the Alpujarras for three days, a medical student
who convinced me that it would be equally sensible
to go to the capital by bus

Why remember the names of these villages?
In Bubión, at the foot of the trail through the cotton flowers and thistle.
Scaled intensities that fill the page with lacing, unlacing: sans serif, curve and stem.

I tasted cheesecake as rich as any I had ever eaten
in the days of my Schwärzwälder youth.

Treasure her prospects and the good fortune of those whom she will heal.

Bizcas

All night I rehearsed a triple murder
The perfect crime
like counting sheep
without a sense of gain

Descartes preferred crossed-eye women.

The Cartuja of Granada

Swirling cascades, jetting fountains that sprout from a spiraling axis in a profusion of
    multiplying vectors, continuing as overlapping foliage with calyxes of fleshy flora, in
    each niche a face, an infant Jesus, a mirror that catches a ceiling populated with angels
    who express their musicality in Tiepolo blues and pinks.

The marble of the floor and columns is burgundy cream, swirled like coffee or cinnamon
    drizzled on steamed milk. At the foot of the hill, the white parroquia
    resembles a mission church in a desert corner of the American Nevada.

Arabesque

Scaled Intensities

Poems from

Jardín Cerrado
Emilio Prados

Final Shadow

Night awakens
like a great wall of stone
and time is pushing it
without being able to demolish it ...
Stars hang
on one side to sustain it:
the sun, from behind, supports it
with hands of glass;
water makes itself into a flag
and the wind a stanchion,
in order to better defend her
against her rival
whose determination does not cease ...

All changes its course;
for night will not end
unless she attains her destiny.

In front of her wall, raised
crosswise, I await my fate:
a gun shot in the silence,
a target in my solitude
that finally completes the mystery
of so much vain searching
for my name in my thought.

Above the wall of night,
in the phosphorescence of sleep
my finger moist with spirit
is writing its sign ...

−Although you see not my body
its life is here, death:
get here quickly, if you are to come.
Spit on my chest
and let your burning saliva
melt me into the black lime
of the shadow of the eternity
that is now supporting me.
Thus will I lose my name
and, in losing it, I hope to attain
what I do not find by thinking
and it is cause of my thinking...
In this sign I await you
and the font for this sign
is my complete knowledge.

Here I am. Don't doubt it any more.
Bring on your blow.

Night awakens
like a great wall of stone
and time pushes against it
unable to demolish it ...
faithful tree of truth,
face to face with night, my body
does not rest from waiting.

My eyes are now morning stars.

On the Earth

I go to sleep in you, upon death, earth;
upon your life, I close, press my eyes
as if I were dead.

The world weighs on me,
as does time
and even the sure beauty
of the human heart.

But I also look up into the tree:
that branch, so tender,
pressed by the sky; in its lap
leaf jabbing leaf,
its fine stem plunging
against the blue flesh
of the wind that rocks it,
if not with the same rhythm
–sometimes more cautious in its way–,
with the same zeal with which it pursues,
snatches and devours the animal, in the end,
its prey won.

So, today, I feel your summer in me,
like a sorrow or a hollow
and I sleep in you
upon death, earth.

I think about my body and see,
only an eye of dark shadow, and, within,
your own death;
as in a dream, so fertile and so pure.
like the deep birth
of water, that, in your unknown veins,
mixes
to refresh the burning pulp
that already, like a shadow
–in the midst of death–, surrounds
the incandescent bone
–captive light, possibly soul–
life of your apple.

All that is dead, in you is able to give life:
the wheat, the blue water,
the pale body of man, fire ...

All can be born

and be dead again
in the same fleeting moment,
in which they call
men free,
fire flame,
reflection light,
wheat grain,
spring transparent water.

Later they may also
live eternally joined
or be eternally dead, together.

But the death in me searches its life.
I know it, because I am a man
and today I fear, in this summer,
earth, the sorrow.

And so I seek
and sleep in you, earth, like a son,
the smallest, the last
but also the most like you
in your presence, mother:
in the august truth
held in your lap.

Insomnia

Who violates my body with blows of an ax
upon this imperfect temple, jarring the world?
What unlit desolation illuminates anguish,
the fevered spirit that throbs in its vein?

Thinking hurts me, naked and agitated
rendering me, drop by drop, all night, unconscious.
Drop by drop, the wound oozes constantly,
upon a sheet of sand, meat of useless earth.

What sin does death bury in the skin of day?...
What heavy chain rolls it in shadow?
I do not know where my dream immolates its new people;
where the town spills beyond its limits, irrational.

It left me at the edge of sleep
beside an abyss, half body leaning out,
with eyes open, hair hanging,
face to face with the idle nullity of time.

I do not know where the timid moon rises;
do not know what new image illuminates me in its desert;
what sin pursues my eyes that lack inherited traits,
what exile sterilizes the reason of my blood...

I am lost in an infinite basket,
without contact and without hope of ordering my sadness.
I do not know –did I say it? – the dream, it is not the land of my people.
I do not know where oblivion coils
the future birth of my life...

                    (The night in her swamp,
luridly presses herself against me in search of my waist...
Slowly, the star begins to deny its flesh
and the slow Universe gives way to Nothing.)

Facing the large and horrible negation of the future,
my desire flares up more anxiously.
My love crumbles and asks the emptiness:
–For whom is this image that my blood now mimics?

....

(My birth flees...

Does the world die with me?...)

The absent throng presses me between the hours.

Part II: Diario mexicano

Mexico: tiempos mezclados

The crystal reveals a direct time-image and no longer an indirect image of time deriving from movement. It does not abstract time; it does better: it reverses its subordination in relation to movement. Giles Deleuze, *Cinema 2: The Time Image.*

.... a cylinder, inscribed with memories,
a ragged weave,
threads like trails of frosted sperm.
Clutter sealed, immemorial,
Notes that ring with sharp brilliance.
I should have begun before things had names;
instead I sorted postcards.
Of cayenne peppers, newly gathered,
three women in lemon and lavender, peppermint creams,
    the molded forms of their haunches, further back
    was a dream
    inscribed links between Nahuatl and Navajo peoples,
    stone calendars.
Also, inexplicably, a photo of an expedition to Lovewell Mtn.
with my daughter and our tireless hunting dog,
looking out on valleys scouted by the mountain's bounty hunter namesake
who lies in the Dunstable burying ground, South Nashua,
as if dispassionate fate had chosen to forge a unity between Thoreau's *Concord and Merrimack*
    and this project, diary of intercut Mexican spaces.
Prepare by evoking an ancient, unacknowledged courtesy.
'Acechar' to stalk.
One of several Joans winces, wide-eyed. The tip of a knife pricks her cheek.
Our age shrouded in new medievalisms of Christian pitted against infidel,
People scamper like rabbits in a painting by Titian,
Sacred Love and Profane, to celebrate a bad resurrection
"detestable pintura" (wrote Julio Cortázar) ...

Ofrenda: animal shells from the sea that feeds us
Seed corn and the bones of a child
In accordance with the Mayan long count, the millennia will end Dec. 23, 2012.
The coffin lids removed; the contents inventoried by angels.

Sor Juana, Her words addressed to Neptune:

Here by inspiration, Providence,
without ending, erect this scaffold
that it might receive from his holy hands
the perfection that is the templo mexicano

Zócalo: temporal notes

In *Neptuno allegorical* the world is understood as a hieroglyphic representation of the Divine will. For Sor Juana, Neptune is a face of the son of Isis, a representation of wisdom. Her text stipulates proportions and design for a triumphal arch to be erected at the Catedral Metropolitana in order to celebrate the entrance into the city of the *virrey*, don Tomás de la Cerda, marqués de la Laguna. My allegory includes fishing boats discovered in their aesthetic perfection when I came first upon the Gulf waters. San Miguel Arcángel, where are your santitos? Preoccupied crowds encounter the desolation of tidal scenes: themes of inundation and protection.

Rivera's murals

in the Palacio Nacional express a brutal history, identifying hope
with recovery of an indigenous humanity.
México en la historia, perspectiva: el campesino oprimido, 1935.
Recovered artifacts sited among the flower beds in his gardens
compose a sacred allegory:
a world constructed of layered forms, blocks of indelible language, incised faces.
Stamps or seals in series. The nation
and its cultures, a project, both political and aesthetic
in its shaping stratagems, unresolved, incomplete.
Cosmological but incomprehensible counterfoil:
Xipe who wears a tunic of human skin.
Decapitation when the play of the ball went counter to the direction of the sun,
competing judges, enthroned each end of the court, guardian spirits.
A bone xylophone, Teponaxtle, played in sacred sacrifice,
bodies of kings and offspring
strewn over the grounds
at a Jonestown in Guyana,
limestone caverns in Bonampak and Laguna.

San Miguel Arcángel, I hear your piping rhythm,
in the calls of vendors, the drumming
of traffic, the shrill notes that signal permission to cross.

Frida stands impassive and some sing hymns.
Huelga, labor actions at industrial sites: Land and Liberty!
Slaughter, rape, execution of unredeemed natives.
Totem animal presences resist the armored crush of horse and pike,
Zapatista women with children slung on their backs.
México is a mestizo nación. It is a caste conscious nation.
The church on the corner of Avenida 20 de Noviembre is San Miguel Arcángel.
México, profoundly a Christian nation, more so than I had anticipated.
México is an indio nation, make no mistake.
A resurgence of copper bodies fills the calles of the capital.
and the small pueblos
with their trash strewn margins.
Three figurines on the sloping wall of the *Templo mayor,*
        attentive and within earshot of the drumming on the Zocaló.

Ballet en Bellas Artes

Clover, shining athlete's body, slender and sensuous hips,
poised in windows and mirrors
that reflect black limbs against a yellow floor, eyes
and teeth wide with welcome.
And the years dissolve.

Doubled

exile
in Calle de Lerma,
confined
in small rooms
with solitude,
he took his sons on walks
in Chapultepec
among
towering
poplars.
They gazed
upon the murals
in the Castillo,
remains of
a continuing
revolution.

Villancicos on my headset

Sansabeya gugurumbé ... a negrilla composed by Mateo Flecha (1482-1553), the sacred context contains percussive African elements and words of Bantu and Yoruba origin.

Standing in endless lines in an anonymous airport, I came face to face with gods and avatars in the person of a Christian woman, horrified by my recounting of human sacrifice among the Aztecs. The ocean itself turns a mass of tide-mauled bodies into a retablo as delicately composed of veiled and tangled forms as any by Agostino di Duccio.

The *Matrículo de Tributos* specifies the amount and kinds of tributes to be delivered to the capital by the varying regions of the empire. It is a business document that speaks to a lifestyle: quantities of beans, corn, feathers.

The relation between form and number, repetition and sequences, variations and accent, are integral to language and vision.

---

no podía morir porque aguardaba
and only 16 years old
a human head emerges from the coiled serpent

Tribute

Among the bales of fiber and chests of honeycomb,
brilliant zigzags, woven stuff to drape the human form, but who watches,
arms crossed, keeper of tributes
and with multiple faces?

My desire was brocade or appliqué, fine details,
shining threads, I found these on dolls
sold in the streets of Mérida and Valladolid, replicas
        of indigenous costumes,
        as in the anthropological museums.
From artisans who made hammocks or their agents,
warehouses and racks of blankets and crockery, with Mayan or Aztec emblems,
offerings not to be despised for possessing consumer value.
So many children with shining eyes holding their mother's hands.

I asked about the lives and homes of those who sought to trade with me, a weaver
        from Temozón, a Totanaca woman from Veracruz.

so many hands have touched the walls in that chamber
Hands soothing a fever, hands pressing like a migraine on the eyeballs,
gray graminaceous organelles,
hands of lovers
and of fathers and daughters
darkly gleaming.

Ceremonial notes:

The sacrificial knife, placed in the mouth, so as to enter the throat
Xipe, the priestly alb of human skin

There is a female aspect of the serpent god, Quetzalcoátl
The penality befalls those who misplay the ball, ullamalitzli

One tochtli: two rabbit or one bowl of pulque
promotes lactation
Centzon totochtin, as mad as 400 rabbits

Merry was a sailor, pulque in Spain, octli in México, gored by a yearling bull
on Dogtown Heath. Of the night sky, Olson wrote:

"She is the heavenly mother
the stars are the fish swimming
in the heavenly ocean she has
four hundred breasts."

The cactus sacred to Mayahuel provides both needle and thread.
Tlaltecuhtli: earth monster, death disk.
She has mouths at her knees and elbows
Her upper half becomes the earth
Her nether parts the sky, from her body come plants that support life.

Xochiquetzal, flower feather.
Coátlicue wears a skirt of snakes and a necklace of her victims hearts.
She is the mother of all creation. Huitzilopochtl born fully armed from her belly,
slew his four hundred brothers and sisters.

In-breath, bone music

Yet unborn children shape this composition,
    readers to be and subjects of the matter that entwines itself with mine.
Suzanne's evocation and Margarita's grief.
Was it mother or child? dead at her own hand?
The *Faust* of Berlioz in Fuentes's presentation, a predestined love that achieves
    apotheosis and decline on a pre-historic precipice: Irimiru karabrao!
Performed immediately after the Second World War in Bellas Artes,
Inez played Marguerite nude in the transport by choruses of pink and healthy angels
    to the imagined here-after
or simply a black woman on a small island
evokes through surrealism a hope for poetry's realization in the hearts of her children.

Cristo and Jeanne-Claude have unveiled their Gates in Central Park
Saffron fantasies, Chinese kites
This diary loops between notes
    from among the high hills and low mountains of Weare, New Hampshire
    ("Over the Hills and Far Away," John Gay's *Beggars' Opera*)
and solitary wanderings to pilgrimage sites in the Yucatán and Bajío,
My baroque methods
approximate redemptive confusion.
Discontinuous dates,
forms eschewing form
Thump, page by page, elephantine.

In Frida's garden, I considered the purchase of a blue cat.
The Blue House has been shaped as an homage to her talent by a faithful unfaithful husband.
She is present in decorative elements, patents for flatware, small bowls
Café furniture: sunflower yellow chairs with tangerine and olive finials.
Her beds have mirrors in the canopies
A retablo: Marxism heals.
A staircase of cards like prayers
inscribes fond sentiments.
Get well, my angel
Cats in the garden,
Cat dishes behind the mock templo.
Aztec and Olmec heads among the greenery
Ollas gigantes for grain and olive oil
Mystical gray glaze, marine forms entangled with the light.
Tanguey and a Klee, paisajes with similar tonalities.
Evidence of independence?
Who is the woman with long lips and a wide mouth, her perfect teeth?
Of the two Fridas, the white one has an open heart,
not like a Saint's, but displayed with surgical precision,
the one transfusing to the other, mother to herself.
The Albright Knox has an autorretrato with a monkey
perched on her shoulder, a sea shell collar around her neck, 1938.

585 days in the cycle of Venus
Fuente de sabiduría.
I sit on a blue cushion, cerulean.

Remember in Coyoacán! We shared Turkish coffee on a second story
balcony overlooking the ornamental garden
The bandstand and eager throng.
How you laughed with the children,
no tiene la culpa el indio, because the Indians were not to blame;
then they raffled off the tequila and you won the one-liter jug of amber gold,
your gringo embarrassment, amusing and humbling.
la pastorela más comíca

Among the bodies from Banda Aceh, torn and shattered boards, a mattress, weeds,
a serving platter, the sheen of drying mud, rendering naked form transparent,
a cataclysm such as Agostino might have rendered it in marble
for the Tempio at Rimini. The body startled from sleep struggles for breath,
as the tide swamps tangled forms, driving the open mouth into the gasping mud.

Tidal forms

Can aquamarine boats or the House of the Seven Dolls speak to this?
Scaling the night sky to assess observable fates, looking under the sun glare
at the remorseless draw and flood of the tropical waves, seeking
signs of life on the deserted Gulf coast.

Fragments of bone, stone masks and skulls with teeth of snail and cowry shell.
The guardian sleeps, in a stupor, after the bout of madness
Beads of agate and jade
Forms or presences
from the sea and earth, now open to the sun,
starkly naked offerings.
The ritual blade in the open mouth.

Hanai, Betus, hulls of Van Gogh turquoise,
Sea-washed Mayan jade at Dzibilchaltun, writing the measures on flat stones,
the observatory at the far end of the eight hundred meter causeway.
Some virgins carry boats in their arms, the bow sprit jutting,
as indigenous women carry ceremonial boats on their heads,
baskets for melons in Tehuantepec, shoulder baskets for sheaves of grain,
in step with the pilgrimage tune, San Miguel Santitos.

Retablo: genocide

Pedro de Alvarado, tasked by Antonio de Mendoza, Vice-regent of New Spain, who had mounted expeditions to find the Seven Golden Cities of Cibola (Wichita, Kansas possibly included) and who also founded the Colegio de Santa Cruz de Tlateloco in 1536 and the Royal and Pontifical University of Mexico, came upon resistance in the jungles of Guatemala and caused all inhabitants to be slaughtered.

In the overlay of log and bone,
a reflection of the turning
cosmological tide.

In the hilltop jungle,
a swinging of machetes against the onslaught of pike
and armored bodies.
Here the naked form
rides above a history whose course
only now begins to break on prophesized shores.

■**TAILANDIA** Dos pequeños descansan sobre un colchón rescatado de su devastada casa

REUTERS

Children

from villages in the region
fill the streets and plazas.
The shop girl imagines
a different glamour but returns
to her parents' house, dutiful.
Grandmother's has one light bulb,
a faded quilt stretched over the window
against the night chill, an open fire in the yard.
Television and the sewing machine
draw current from one wire.
To improve rural sanitation, provide
additional facilities. Many simply
shit in the fields. Everywhere I have been
the elderly like to rub their hands and arms
and enjoy the brightness of a fire,
a glow on their faces. The young
take the colectivo at dawn, at noon
under plane trees, embracing,
her lips scented vanilla and pear blossom,
ignore parodic stunts, circus acts.
Silent statues, unmoved,
when dancers crowd the bandstand.
The brown people do not inhabit
the white mansions, many
now hotels for tourists. I do not
give to the cripple in the doorway
as freely as the poorest might.
Carts and foodstands crowd the walks,
a bounty of roast meats, fruit cups, footwear,
bathing goggles, confusedly on offer.
The city, a mosaic of interpenetrating spaces,
resistant to the passage of buses and trucks,
nothing felt or seen so noxious or rancid
as to cause hesitation. Shell of baroque ruins.
An impulse to rest against a sunny wall
and photograph human forms:
vendors and their children, close together,
boarding a bus. Mapmaker poet
swept up, inundated.

Baroque ruins

DEC. 30, Mérida, a city with its own Ballet Folklórico, poetry and music, so claimed the Master of Ceremonies, has, through its support of the arts, resisted globalization; much visited because, unlike other regional capitals, it has not been absorbed into a generic Mexican identity. Does Yucateca in this context mean Spanish colonial or creole, mestizo or indigene? Not the time for answers. White linen costumes, hems embroidered with roses and marigolds, the performance of El torito has a peninsular source; other routines ironize the ability of labor to perform dexterous feats, balancing serving trays on heads. Yucatecan boleros represent a continuation of a tradition shared with Cuba, abruptly terminated between 1959 and 1962. At this time, the manufacture of guayaberas began in Mérida. In "Serenata yucateca" the orchestration swings with 1940's moon light. The Master of Ceremonies might well have said that Mérida has preserved a quality of culture lost to most regions in their rush to modernize, an authentic modernism with Latin roots. The throng as it applauds, shifts in texture from white to mestizo. The Orquestra Jaranera de Mérida is neither a mariachi nor a ballroom ensemble in its presentation of itself. Imagine the cigar smoke in their club rooms, the gleam of brass of the horns in unison. The young contralto finds the old men in their white jipis to be charming. Imagine a public recital of poetry, a toast to the mothers and the girls who danced in the gardens and a lost childhood, moving us all to histrionic tears.

On the metro in México, a child followed his brother who played cumbias on the accordion; another child sold those ignition sticks used to light a gas burner. Here the children carry baskets of sugary sweets, working the enraptured throng. Cultural difference does not lie in any detectable economic superiority. Here and in the metropolis alike, a sense of a people collectively asserting their desire to transform the stakes.

The hotel, El Fray Diego, emulates the most antique engagement with the Mayan people, rooms arranged like cells around the courtyard: altars and religious paintings, crucifixes on key rings. Fray Diego Landa, among his accomplishments in his mission of conversion, betrayed a fascination with Mayan sacrificial ceremonies. After the holocaust, the economy still turns on that wheel, fascination with dimly felt mystery.

Uxmal

Two times to Uxmal, its dovecote and macaw's roost,
impossibly recursive. On the first return, unexpected confidence
in my abilities to navigate: jarring topes in the road.
Identity papers, passport and the required
folleto de migración turística,
mislaid, not where I expected to find them
on my return to my room,
compromised self, panic at the old year's end.
No magical purpose at work here or in the recovery.
Near noon, I had been splayed on a high platform
for a sun god's inspection,
exposed post-operative on offer.
On the lawn of the palace, jewel box
of ancient authority, children played at jaguar
and diviner. From my perch I examined
the bedrooms where girls feted before sacrifice.
Fields and shrub forests in the distance,
remarkably green toward the north coast.
Do they burn the earth to destroy the thorn bushes,
potentilla fruticosa, morning glory, red darts of a fennel
where I trespassed upon uncharted ruins?
Descending the ninety-nine stairs,
a small incautious boy tottered
on the brink of a well. I called out, "¡Cuidado!"
Happily, he did not fall. I acquired a guidebook to Mayan ruins
with reprints of drawings by Catherwood
and daguerreotypes by Charnay. Also a puppet,
with an arm long sleeve, wearing
typical yucateca costume. And a jipi.
No great awakening in these details,
only that my tourism seemed almost joyous,
setting aside, for reasons of conscience, my status:
consumer without identity in an impoverished land.
At night, on the second return, error led me into Muná,
known for workshops that specialize in reproductions.
Museum security had recovered my papers
from the floor of a stall where I had urinated,
dislodging the passport from a waistband
when extracting bills. With my papers restored,
I was able to view the sound and light show,
son et lumière, turning to my left (so often I take
the long way around), assuming that on this night,
naturally, I might be one of only a few there,
gingerly stepping over grates
that house flood lights, then turning, about face,
to find myself on the opposite side of the quadrangle

from the crowded stands on the north wall, "Chac, Chac"
stereo prayers to end the drought.
Quetzalcoatl, his form wound among the Puuc friezes,
illuminated blue, then green. How can I explain
that the serpent god has female aspects? Venus, Lucero?
On this night, I had intended to meet my scorpion woman,
my Shango, Santa Barbara. Endless New Year's Eve
dawning on a desolate balcony overlooking
an empty plaza, supping on cream of cilantro soup,
desiccated *poc-chuk*, the white carriages waiting to transport
lovers to balls in mansions on Avenida Montejo.

In the Christian era, John The Baptist assumes the mantel of Chac. Classic Mayan
religious concepts endure. The "Black Christ" known as the Señor de Tila is an amalgam
of Christ and Ik'al, a Precolumbian cave-dwelling earth deity report Nicholas Hopkins and
Kathryn Josserand of Florida State University

Among the Quiché of highland Guatemala, says Barbara Tedlock, a State University of
New York, Buffalo, anthropologist and trained shaman-priest, "some illnesses can even be
a call to serve gods and ancestors." There are six such illnesses—snake, horse, twisted
stomach, dislocated bone, inebriation, and money loss—all of which incapacitate a
patient. To cure them requires becoming a daykeeper, one who burns incense and offers
prayers at shrines on designated days of the *tzolkin*, the 260-day sacred calendar.

Confession

Here then is the truth of New Year's dawn:
Continue, you can go on!
The city again alive!
A crowd overflowed the portal
of the basilica, San Ildefonso,
vendors and beggars among believers.
I sat to the back with a young family.
We sang. I prayed a few words
in a Spanish that seemed church Latin
and wondered back to my deep resistance
against the sacrilege that I might do. Communion
without confessing to thievery, falling
from sin into indiscretion, because
of untrammeled lust, normal
to a boy my age then, weighing yet
as embarrassment now
after so many years of exile
from holiness. My only claim:
I felt whole for a fleeting moment
when the brown-eyed girl
clasped my hand. I saw her pain.
She wanted no more from me.
I had no more to give.
Nostalgia expended.

cuahutli, águila

Writing in a Cuban café, after settling questions regarding room, I mull travel options: Valladolid and Río Lagarto. I imagined stone faces emerging from the flowering vines, orchids. In the villages around Progreso, sulfurous mud turned the marsh growth bone gray. Charred trash littered the wetlands. Unburnt plastic sacks, bright oranges and blues, caught on the branches of fire resistant shrubs. Childhood memories of warm turquoise Caribbean water impelled me toward Tulúm.

For me it was wonderful to embrace briefly and feel your inner strength and beauty. I understand it was not a completely joyous afternoon for you. Ana Mendieta's work opens intense vulnerabilities. Terrain you know better than me. I felt your need for freedom— redundant now to say that you were already free. So many people will continue to place demands on you and you will choose to comply. Silence, no alternative, opposes the writer's drive. We are very much face to face at this moment. Together, we explore time and space, enter the world of well-springs that cease not to flow, altars sacred to jaguars.

---

from Sonetos

The son that the slave girl conceives,
so says the law, belongs
to that legal guardian who owns her
of whom the child is born

Inkblots, offered
Incautious deception of sentiments
Inept counterfoil to fate:
corpse, shadow, dust, nothing
                Sor Juana Inés de la Cruz

Kuanon of the market

Not her, but another. I saw briefly in the crowd.
She disappeared between the columns
of a market more ancient than Mérida.
Entered the cave
                    and swam in the cold well water.
She met me on the grassy lawn,
having traveled from China, her eyes
pearls of jade, merciful Kuanon,
helpful not judgmental

On the paths between sacred sites
precisely where
flayed virgin remains
filled the cistern
were displays for pilgrims, abundant
masks and retablos, solar disks,
miniature pyramids of brilliant hues
in plastic and hand-carved forms

Attention to detail
imbues the object
with magical authority.
The carnival play of the vendors
who occupy winding paths
among monuments,
their presence, integral to sacred space,
as are gothic athletes who ascend
the ninety stairs, ornamental
to the serrated edges of the temple.

Tulúm

Happier I will be at Tulúm, sacred to honey bees
Where the god descends into the sea
My purpose on that cliff, as at an earlier time,
to experience disorientation
Multiple languages revolve in my mind
Taste the sacred mushroom, the bowl of pulque
and meet her destined lips

I drove miles over the vast plain, fleeing holiday crowds.
Arid fields with the persistent burning of refuse at the margins.
Plastic bottles on branches to mark the turns for farms and campsites.
The land being rich in underground rivers, natural wells water the rock.
A question in that circumstance with respect to the decline of civilizations.
Armed invasion will override immediate economic cause.
At the turning onto the main highway from the Coba road,
young soldiers force me to step from my car.
My ear does not catch the full meaning of their words.
They are impatient, in newly pressed uniforms
and black M-16's click against their shoulder straps.
The dark smell of gun oil, as cars and trucks speed by.

Valladolid

O, Valladolid of song, my refuge, famous for the inception
of the *Guerra de castas,* purveyor of meats in *pibil* and honeyed *calabaza*
Cumbias and dancing for all ages, every Sunday, in the jardín
Deeply thankful to find access through an arco iris to the carpark.
My projection alone that anyone was anxious at all.
The revolution now underway occurs in the bellies
of Mayan woman, pregnant multitudes,
destined to reclaim the land.
Children excited about the holidays, candies and incense,
diminutive pastores, holding tinfoil crooks,
cheered by coronets, triumphant angels,
syrupy sweet drinks everywhere available,
roast meats prepared on sidewalk grills.
In Valladolid, I imagine world peace to be possible,
seeing the many brides, horny bastard,
I ask myself, is it so wrong that in these circumstances
a priest embraces chastity? A transparently suffering,
grandmother stepped cautiously over the threshold of the church,
her hips bothering her, then a mother with bared breasts
entered from the nursery garden. The women
carry their bellies high on strong legs.
Last year 1.5 million tourists visited the Yucatán
whose population is 2 million. Three times as many women
as men marry before the age of 18. 1,559 in 2004.
Diario de Yucatán, 3 enero 2005.
The Spanish appreciated the proximity of the Yucatán to Cuba.
Fisgono, the nosey waiter wants to know what I am writing.
Garza, the imperial heron. Whose fantasy is Thalia or Pau,
how not violate a child? the schoolgirls parading through the park?
Even their mothers are children. Her sister walks with her
between the carts and clowns, beggars and men
with crinkly eyes. The fountain, a china doll
in her misty elegance, a moment
to catch the breath on the way home.
The grandmother on the portico of San Bernardino
does not turn to me or acknowledge
my desire to talk. A story teller
who wanders from tribe to tribe,
I record the births and deaths of inevitably
tangled lineages. The news I have has been heard before,
an acceptance that originates in the long view
of how determinative points intersect
on the wheels turning within wheels.

A cosmic rhythm sweeps through the dancing throng,
some brown, one white with incisive eyes and a beard sculpted by Van Dyck.
Easily a swordsman in a past life.
People of so many shapes and color that my instinct
is to protect myself by merging continuously
with disparate forms.
Who will survive if the earth's axis
receives a knock, jarring it more significantly
than did the Indian Ocean terremoto?

Río Lagarto

Water, milky with sulfurous mud, *lodo maya*, with which I paint my face,
washed away with my baptismal plunge into the sweet water *cenote*.

The boatman understood flamingoes, promised
crocodiles among bone-gray mangroves,
victims of tormentas
in the hurricane season. The green to return
with the full round of the sun.

Gaviotas, gannets and herons, garzas feed in the shallow waters

My pilgrimage coracle spins round
off the deserted strand of Las Coloradas.
Holidays end, 3 January 2005.
Crossing the plank bridge,
pelicans and boys eye one another.
Erratic gypsy weaving
between shore and field, rich in reflective habitats,
mirages on sun-baked roads.

The horizons and rancheros of the coast
display majesty in their colonial scale;
herds, fields of sisal,
counterpose the dust from limestone crushing machinery.

The Convent of San Bernardino

I wandered from the classroom of the cloister
into the brothers' garden
I saw the drying pottery, peppers and aromatic herbs,
the cabinet of small caskets in a side chapel.
A warden led me to the bell tower.
I saw the sacred suffering
in simple stark detail.
For all the history of pain and hatred
inscribed on its charred walls, the monastery
has become a family center, sacred to a Madonna
who is herself a doll in a pretty dress.
The underground spring, a life-giving well.

Dusty side roads of gravel and chalky clay, piedra y sahcab
walking sideways through an intersection from schoolyard to the zócalo
in one of many villages between Valladolid and Mérida,
some linked by ancient causeways.

                                        Inspecting the flowers, vegetables,
caught by the splendor of hibiscus that hangs from white walls,
looking into a dark interior, space for a hammock
or a cane bottom chair.
To sit at the dominoes table,
hits of hard liquor
in the cantina, brawling, not my part, not in this video my life.

Looking for a work space to work when possible to work, to carry away an object made there, a heavy
object that weighs so the arms pull down, pull down from the socket where the shoulder aches, ache
again with a dull flame, dull stone, unyielding in its ageless sorrow that pulls from a distance as
gravity does, longing to be consumed by the volcano as salt sweat beads on the stone.

Izamal

Catholic and Mayan Yucatán meet at Kinich Kak Mo, sacred
to the sungod, maker, modeler, bearer, begetter, Itzamná,
avatar of the Madonna of Izamal.
The Convent of Saint Anthony of Padua, founded upon
the ruins of one of several pyramids, by his excelencia,
primero Obispo yucateca, Fray Diego.
In Izamal, at the turning of the Catholic millennium,
indigenous peoples assembled in his name.
She is the moon, Ixchel; he is the sun.
Virgen de Izamal, the female face of god
Banquet tents set for a wedding.

Zamná, dios inventor de la escritura y descubridor de la fibra del henequén y sus beneficios.

That night, an Indian couple entered the refectory,
he with a tom-tom tuned as deep as any bass drum, she with a tambourine.
Outside their grandfather played Gabriel's horn.
3114 the origin of the cosmos, 3121 the forming of the mother goddess.

Xquiq passed by a tree of forbidden fruits, and picked one of the fruits. The gourd she chose
was the head of Hunhun-Apu. He told her not to fear him for she would bear a child soon.
When her father heard of this, he sent four owls to slay her and bring her heart back to him
in a vase. She convinced the owls not to harm her, but instead to bring not her heart, but
the coagulated sap of the bloodwort plant, back to her father. Xquiq went to Xmucane, the
mother of Hunhun-Apu, for protection. At first Xmucane did not believe the girl's story but
the two women soon grew close, and it was not long until Xquiq gave birth to Hun-Apu and
Xbalanque.

Marriage

Norma Inés Cimé Chan se consagra a la vida religiosa
And I was there in Izamal. Looking from the balcony of St. Anthony of Padua, you are so good
with children, she said at a different time, serving me coffee and her pregnant sister joking about
who spoke better Spanish or Italian.

The temple mount, rubble and lavender,
emerging above corrugated roof tops.
From this balcony, the dying (dead) Pope gave his message
                to the peoples of the Americas,
                castigated clergy
                who preached liberation.
No violence in the Name of God
Now Inés with her sisters sings the marriage hymns,
a chorus of guitars and priestly droning.
Citizens from the Chinese Mayan quarters of the world
        celebrate her day.
Local identity, even more than national, springs from the adoration of the Virgin,
one or several mysteries: creamery complexion,
a hint of brown or rose, yellow as the light changes.
All women are sacred, the men sing, smoothing the mortar
to patch the gold walls of the convent.
Virgen de Izamal, face of god
writing numbers,
summing apocalypse.

Penitence

turned away because I had violated
her established presence,
one of the parcas
at this gate
since the beginning.

For her, in her sacred age, having outlived generations of children,
the flash of the camera is too painful for the soul to bear,
voyeuristic rape that shames me.
The body of the mother repeatedly violated.

Sinner, can you not enjoy the simple elegance,
of how the clothes
move with the frail frame.
Each type her own floral veil,
embroidered hem, each her station among the dolls and madonnas.

An Elegguá, call from the mountaintop, accepting
the sacrifice of children.
The blues singer on his knees
knows that life is short
with respect to the long count.
Pilgrimage leads
through animistic acts of volition,
from the coastal plain
by bus and foot to the Bajío.
Lost en route, poems, *El Jardín Cerrado*,
that I wanted to understand,
misplaced, at café table
left behind in a monastic cell.
May the loss serve
as restitution for recoveries.

In streets named for rivers,
I fail to find the poet's home.
He found refuge here
for children in political exile
in a time of civil war.
The music that I collect
for a personal imaginary
reflects displacement.

My fear and personal revulsion
at tyrannical politics
does not carry weight
with those who fill the streets
and bus terminals.
Better to keep silent
and to myself. Tourists
will fall first, even those
who fade into the throng.
Skin receivers have seen it before.
The new plastic models
are not fire resistant.

The voice of Elena Burke suffused the spirit of Gabriel García Márquez as he wrote his *El amor en los tiempos de cólera.* According to an article in *El Universal,* he enjoys the parodic reality of *La oreja,* a show that I watch on Telemundo. Colorful materials that so delight children, balloons and pull toys, doll babies too, become in time or after burning, brittle and indestructible char. Use humor to inoculate against another holocaust; crystal meth against boredom. Laughter or misery? What trumpet or sword will signal Judgment Day in the Christian west? Calendrical evidence of a dissociative disorder, an inability to negotiate the streets? 400 rabbits!

San Miguel Arcángel

With my propensity to take frequent wrong turns, I found several centers en route from the hotel in Guadiana to the illuminated towers of the Parroquia of San Miguel Arcángel. I stumbled on the remote well, outside the old walls, where early inhabitants, guided by Fray Juan de San Miguel, drew water and planted fields of grain. Among convolutions of place names and saint's names, "San Miguel ... santito, santito" recurs bright like the clicking heels of children who parade on cobblestones, tempo unvarying, the small drum with a tin rattle to its tympanum. A mother said, "They do not tire."

Baroque splendor

Despite its altitude, San Miguel de Allende lies under the eternal haze of the central valley.
In some neighborhoods, English is spoken more readily than Spanish.
Tourists will die. There will be no exceptions.

Honor trade as a way of life, ancient market customs
Is it not pleasure in abundance that enhances survival?
the smiles of children? Waste and contamination
controlled by burning. The change is in the nature
of materials, plastics and acetates.

Yes, the power of the poor inundates the streets
and a people not yet born inhabit the huts and temples,
witness the joy in celebration of Los tres reyes.

Crema del corazón. A poor man's lunch
with lightly dressed tuna.

How meticulously so many things are done, fussing with details
and yet a tolerance for disorder,
singing on cue but then scrambling one over another pell mell.
The priest who bears the host,
the entourage of bearded magi and the children who stop at each altar
to pray to the virgin whose body lies on her glass-encased bier
Tin foil wrapped shepherd's crooks, flowers, harps,
and cardboard crowns swirl, clamor and fall
as the chorus intones endlessly
  "María llena de gracia."
Hail Mary, Hail Mary, Hail Mary,
kneeling unobtrusively with the parents
I must smell of incense myself.

In a restaurant famous for it churros, I stare at a baby's butt.
The cherub offers a cafecito to San Augustin,
seeming parody of other baroque aspects of San Miguel de Allende.
The food here shares that quality
of excessive preparation
that distinguishes the baroque.
Think only of the facades: Oratorio de San Felipe Neri or San Francisco.

'Pechuga de pollo' – chicken folded around a layer of spinach
and arugula, breaded, smothered in a green mole.

Mothers and children like birds

A woman feeds doves from her fingers
and they flock to my table
As if in Rapallo, children wheeling across a plaza,
the shadows of birds.
Notes on a staff at Las Musas.
The sap of aguamiel has an nutritive effect, aids lactation,
writes Oswaldo Goncalves de Lima

Thistle seed attracts humming birds
Guamare and Purépecha inhabited the mountains before
        the Spanish arrived, following the trails to the silver mines

Marketing enters the imagination
as a fascination
to those children whose mothers
bring them to the Jardín. It is in the blood,
the stories that people tell, their amusements.

Does manufacturing cloth or leather
also fascinate
the cross-legged child
sitting at a loom with crippled feet
or endlessly sanding
mahogany mask, salad bowl, totem.

Totaneca market woman in the jardín

I wanted to speak at greater length
Her life and home?
Her child was shy.
Her costume like that of her dolls,
a selling point.
I read in her eyes sure knowledge
of who will die first.
Once more, her children
        will inherit the earth.

My eyes scan

flagstones, their uncanny fit, rose gray
wedges and petals. There are murals in the parroquia de San Miguel
depicting the conversion of the Chichimecas. The colors coming together,
shards fitted to a perspective, enforced prostration
Hunters and gatherers who practiced agriculture in the river valleys.

On an evening

in New Hampshire, I slice citrus. Fresh juice has become a fetish,
sipped from a wine glass. My mornings are too hurried,
now that I am teaching.
I set the table with tangerine and lemon yellow china
made incidentally in Mexico.
The pattern is pleasing. I find patterns
among elements tossed together, verbal ensaladas
A sketch of a possible score in several parts: birds that share my thoughts,
dolls and pottery
glazed with a perfect azure of Pueblo origin.

The song is an intimation of an end,
how a world that cannot not be sustained will find itself overturned
in a human tumult. Learn now
to appreciate a simple transition, a fortunate interim
in which to meditate upon dishes and beverages.

In the Alameda

The dark beer is smooth, not bitter like some European products. I am paging through a catalog for an exhibition of the works of Miguel Covarrubias, subtitled *Retorno a los Orígenes*. An artis unknown to me before this evening's walk. I had come this way on this night in order to view Rivera's monumental, *Sueño de una tarde dominical en la Alameda Central*. Frida's plumed ha competes with that of La Catrina for our attention in an evocation of Seurat, blending mestizo culture with the Sunday parade of fashionable people. Unlike Rivera's search for authentic sources of modern life, authentic Mexican forms of modernism, Covarrubias' instincts are more nearly those of an anthropologist. Drawings for his many publications had been mounted in the surrounding galleries. Among other objects were illustrations for Melville's *Typee* and Langsto Hughes's *The Weary Blues*, two texts that continue to shape my sensibilities. In his work in Bal and in his work with Mexican indigenous people, his sense of individual body or costume transcends easy classification of type or social category, in this being more true to human expression than the work of some 19th century photographers.

I found la Casa de los Azulejos, blue ceramic tiles from Puebla, sheathing the façade. Near it th bookstore where I examined several first editions of Covarrubias's work. Mariachi in the Café Tacuba sang birthday songs to patrons, waitresses in white, seemingly nurses, in their efficient service.

Avenida Orizaba

The nineteenth century houses, art institutes and small hotels
of this avenue with its parks and fountains,
its cock proud copy of Michelangelo's David,
feels like a possible home.
A photograph by Manuel Álvarez Bravo
of a woman taking in the wash,
transient elegance and purity
He roamed these streets
and filled his rooms with images
of the working poor and murdered labor activists.
Although there is evidence of prosperity
to be found at many intersections,
grandmothers and children pick over the trash.
Some houses partly swallowed by the earthquake of September 1985
speak to a baroque that transcends
restorative hands.
The epicenter off the Pacific coast generated tsunamis
and the land pulsed with aftershocks.
Still, it is pleasant here, now, gazing on this ruined mansion.

My companion is a truck driver from Querétaro,
employed now in Columbia, South Carolina
by a furniture company. He is well-informed
on world politics and willing to chat about Mexican culture,
in particular his taste in music, cumbias and rancheras,
and his pride in the baroque architecture of his town.
For him, the bonds between indio and mestizo peoples
are simple facts, affecting housing, diet and commerce,
and spiritual health.
In Banda Aceh, two babies who have lost their parents,
lie on a turquoise mattress. In Ceylon,
the man who pulls the girl from the torrent,
rapes her repeatedly. On the borders of the river of mud,
animals bray, screaming their panic; rabbits cry.
El patrón del viaje es el dios del sol.
I had returned to Manchester on the 25th,
after an agony of waiting, because the plane for México
could not depart Charlotte. On the 26th the tsunami
inundated the coasts of the Indian Ocean, from Sumatra to Somalia.
Seek in the New Year, favorable winds, prosperity, Ehecatl, for all children.

Part III: Oaxaca

Expressive artifacts abrupt on felt realities, universes of feeling. My model is Charles Olson's *Mayan Letters*. I am an outsider, participant and observer, traveling through the land, learning how others perceive themselves, discovering new perceptions of my motives and practices.

Earthenware: Oaxaca

Tin-glazed
Four petal compass, stellate
The shoot curls within the pod
Monocotyledon
Horned whelks, honeycomb snails adhere
to the cosmic rim

Charcoal layers
Her skirt sweeps the floor
Ribbed shell
Bared-breasts, wasp woman
of summer skies

Amulets of molded
kernels, exhumed
from crevasse, royal tomb
Sacred ears,
fed on blood, gives human strength
to human gods.

Tropicalia

Did I tell you how
the efflorescence of Tropicalia,
as I experienced it in Chicago,
plunged me into obsessions?
Absorbed by the passage through shoals,
a figure at the mast. What
most remains like love
are costumes, posters, psychedelic hues.
Installations (is the current word "scenographies"?)
Brechtian matter, his *Jungle of Cities*, 1969:
Ítala Nandi performed the first nude scene in Brazilian theater.
"You know that I have written on Cendrars," Odile remarked.
"No, not the New Objectivity."
Magical realism.
Now they teach historic and ecological
re-construction, the arts in service of globalization.
Tourist economies transform the ghetto into old world arcades.
The subject of satire has become the lynchpin of normalization,
the rock guitarist, the Minister of Culture.
The gloss of green with black tiger stripes,
very much the skin each lizard
wants to wear
this season.

I cling to the bowsprit
of my forwarding.

Partial reduction of limits

Unlike the rest of Europe, in all parts of France, an undermining mist, clings to the surface of walls and to the underside of leaves.

« Il y a dans la nature et il subsiste dans l'homme un mouvement qui toujours excède les limites, et qui jamais ne peut être réduit que partiellement. De ce mouvement nous ne pouvons généralement rendre compte. Il est même par définition ce dont jamais rien ne rendra compte. » *(L'Erotisme.)*

Degradation of the biosphere

In an investigation of unformed forms, formless matter, nightmare textures
(my personal Bataille),
eggs and testes are
primary globules,
excrescences, yellow honey.

Figuration

At some point in the present
I begin with matter of recent origin
and reach back to an elsewhere.
Marginal jottings produce observations.
Small deposits left in the act
of going forward:
figurations that shape
present time,
not transforming
the present of the source,
but impelling a future still unfolding.

Block, stunt, twist, or torque
from the filaments of desiring production,
immanence inescapably
asserts itself.

In hop-scotch gear,
the present of any point
is never necessarily a recent point
It is instead a point that catches the eye
because a phosphorescence
once existed, then flares,
"blindspots" amid adjacencies,
vacancies where polyangular
perspectives merge, time in multiple
ordinary senses
transforming space
(inner, more within, outer).

The "figural" abstracts or isolates. "Always between two figures, history glides or tends to glide, animating the illustrated ensemble. To isolate is then the easiest way, necessary although not itself sufficient, to interrupt representation, break to the story-line, impede illustration, liberate the Figure so it attains to its own reality." (Giles Deleuze, *Francis Bacon: Logique de la sensation* 10)

Mariana Yampolsky

author of temples and osarios en el jardín
Clotted nopal
Stones like skulls heaped in the entry
hut
potters shed
under a glorious oak
Dangú, Hidalgo, 1973.
The faces of children mirror a rainless sky, *emotiva mirada*
Calabazas and piñatas fill the frame.
A stucco wall, a study in brown and shades of tan, the window dressed with lace curtains.
Compare her to an envisioning machine
who undermines the limits of seeing.

(Chicago 1925 - Ciudad de México 2002)

Figure / Leonel Góngora

A tenderness

we fail to understand

Think macho or masochist

face to face with her splayed

headless form

His face in a shard of mirror

Platen of sheet metal

like a surgeon's

His smile looking

over the modesty curtain

A cloud of worry

sponge of her flow

The bronzed blade

marked with a smooch

yellow operating table,

signed drippy scrawl:

Lg óng ora

Public arts

At the end of the line, tren ligero,
implicate patronage, Museo Dolores Olmeda Patiño
Personal holdings of baroque and indigenous art
an enabling condition.
Beloved Xoloitzcuintli
and peacocks
wander
Sketches worked into monuments
of emerging national consciousness
Faces and legs and arms
add up
Inventory
of working parts, transformed
Labor and indigenous rights coalesce
Mandate, unresolved
Beyond the sports stadium,
houses of unpainted concrete blocks
Garages, gas stations, sidewalk food stands
in Noria at the end of the tram line.

Reforma

In each cell of the colony, if the application of force exceeds a threshold of vibration ...

¿Eres tu, México, cuna de mi soledad?

Rooms in Reforma
Bar in Condesa
Sweet camarones, as never, salsa de ajo

Learning the quirks of Avenida Hamburgo, confronting at an intersection garish lovers, coarse full lips; then in a children's park inscribed with memories of Leipzig, an alley between office blocks and the carpark, opens on a small plaza with a monument in the presumed likeness of Giordano Bruno, student of poly-angularity, he sought to beautify human nature and human cities in the face of the advance of the apocalyptical beast :

Y dispongamos de tal manera al sol que está a punto de salir, que no nos descubra tan inmundos como estamos, debemos limpiarnos y hermosearnos, no solamente nosotros sin⦁ también nuestras estancias y nuestros techos han de estar pulidos y claros; debemos purificarnos interior y exteriormente.

Expulsion de la bestia triunfante

For a period of 21 months,
to determine the needful equilibrium,
Fernando López Carmona
suspended an enormous pendulum
from the crossing of the dome
of the Catedral Metropolitana.
The Capilla del Altillo is a rhomboid,
its roof, a hyperbolic parabola. Arcs
intersecting angles that spill
over the sun-bright
plazas, precisely indicated
shadows, enormous clocks, radial arms,
define solar scales.

.... barandales de cobre, algunos de manufactura china y otros mexicanos; los guardapolvos de azulejo de las escaleras; las columnas churriguerescas de cantera del patio principal al igual que la fuente con remates de mosaicos; los remates de porcelana francesa del techo, de la fachada de Madero y también la del callejón de la Condesa.

Tepotzotlán

The bells of Tepotzotlán say, be less righteous. Golden city, walls of ochre.
Each oblong of butter hand-wrapped in tissue of corn husk, secured by a bow.
Be less judgmental: each part of the plant has use.
Bells order traffic.
Buses bounce
up the mountain from Rosario, the process
in which you partake.
Breakfast shared with a hornet.
Do not rush thought.
In plaited segments,
pilgrimage song, layers of air.

Each statue of la Guadalupana has a gray face,
no other indications of indigenous masses enslaved by the virrey.
In the parroquia adjacent, a truly attenuated Christ.
From the wound behind his ear, blood runs into the armpit.

My text repeats other texts on the theme of oppression.
Self-accusatory about my bourgeois mysticism, devout before the golden altars.

Not a dark face within the multiple perspectives in the golden Capilla de la Virgen de Loreto,
jeweled house transported from Palestine. In the mirrored Camarín, Archangel Michael, white
warrior, defends the heavens; canopies of stars ride his shoulders. What can be said about the
role of art in creating a national consciousness when its burden is historical fact? To transform
without transport denies blood lore and ritual, enshrines compulsion.

In the market of Tepotzotlán, she sells small plastic umbrellas,
child-sized for a Tres Reyes pleasure.
Offered under the gold tinsel cone of the municipal Christmas tree
are mirrors set in ornate plaster frames, gilded cages for your parakeets.
In the evening light, how the market rivals the dome of San Francisco!

Reading in *La Reforma*, in her daughter's words,
how her husband silenced Elena Garro's advocacy of labor and indigenous rights—
core of necessary identification
cites betrayals
that garrulous men cannot understand.
"La culpa es de los tlaxcaltecas"
Copper hatchet, sign of the inebriated, Tepoztécatl

Gallery

The servers in Casa Azulejos
wear turquoise aprons with rose ribbons,
caps like angel wings.
Sing, I am thankful for the wisdom of Giordano Bruno
who burned at the stake for his beliefs

Fasting on the First Day of 2006,
water scented with a hint of tangerine
I rode to Oaxaca
with a young woman, Mixtec eyes of Siqueiros
She said little and dismounted in the hills
to see her child. ¡Ten cuidado!

The gardener kindly contacted my hostess
How else explain the loss of dollars?
Alrededor de la silla estaban Santa Clauses

Lorena's purse closes with an apple green strap
Green, sweet apples and slices of pineapple interleaved
The cathedral an ivory yellow
in the white light. The dove ascending,
as finale, in the topmost frieze
Woman, he says, is always only a symbol
never is she herself

Elena saw betrayal, returning the woman full circle
to herself in herself for her people
A deep Mexico in danger of extermination

From the produce of the land come stories
now needing telling
How the manner of death
outweighs the value of living

Conception is communal
Doll parts she sang, muñecas plásticas
Red plastic wigs
Two festival queens
Bared breasts of young women bathing in Tehuantepec
charm the railroad passengers,
Covarubbias' image recurs in García Márquez
Revolution's uneasy address to sex.

Poses

Photography has become a photographing of tableaux.
Atget or Alvarez Bravo's ordinary mannequins, surreal in shop windows
Then dolls designed to be photographed, Belmer
     precedes Cherry 2000 (1987)
Forever young: post-apocalyptic parody
Vanessa Beecrofts's parades (fatigue caps in Leipzig, Genoa, São Paolo)
Glass babes with hollow arm sockets, brothers'
     pouting lips raised to the onlooker's gaze (Marta Thoma)
Impassive women await an indefinite call (Phillip-Lorca Dicorcia)
Matte face, beehive hair, transcendent patience
Jenny Gage's Helen holds a gun
My life it stood, the present arms stance
A rifle barrel between feet emblazoned with sacred texts (Sherin Neshat).

Reason why

Cruel thirst, among mountains that divide east from west,
          descending toward Oaxaca, the Pacific haze in a possible distance.
Relentless sun on dust and chalky gravel.
Hallucination of windows reflecting windows
She dismounted at a nameless stop
Among the wind-tossed candy wrappers
impenetrable perimeter.
back to the wall of
a possible home
scouring
the mold from my night sweats

On level 3b no problems exist
So the blonde women from Germany assure me
Muses of the Instituto Cultural
Freely ask about indigenous rights
Practice the subjunctive
Discover I am reading Elena Garro
in her own words.
Those before were her daughter's.
Her husband?
Lamentará alguno mi ausencia
Masculine vanity
The deepest authority is the village
The market enacts possible stories
Songs and legends
recipes and instruction
all coded in the weaving
of blankets and scarves
Tianquis / trueque
Guelaguetza / compartir
Mutual aid is the deep law, gozoma
She walked into dust of her dreams, disappeared child
Xonaxi, our mother

Lesson

Bright vowels carry an accent to distinguish them from diphthongs
Eight days remain
Tamales elote
Tehuántepec has always been a crossing place

in Mexico to be nested more profoundly
within surfaces of mindfulness

Mother of mestizaje, chingara, a slave
spoke Mayan and Nahua, learned Spanish for revenge
16 ethnicities recognized in Oaxaca

La diosa Tonantzín, Madre de la Patria.
Poems produce history
Juan Rulfo, the revolution continues,
Conversation with a ghost,
one sentence in *Cien años de soledad*

Reforms eliminated the civil role of the church
Latifundio, degollando
Zapata: We'll restore what Juárez destroyed

Sin tierra no termina la revolución
Future histories

Colocando en primer plano el problema económico-social, asumimos la actitud menos lírica y menos literaria posible. No nos contentamos con reivindicar el derecho del indio a la educación, a la cultura, al progreso, al amor y al cielo. Comenzamos por reivindicar, categóricamente, su derecho a la tierra.

Placing the socio-economic problem in the forefront, we adopt the least lyrical and least literary attitude possible. We do not content ourselves with reclaiming the right of the Indian to education, to culture, to progress, or to love or heaven. We begin by reclaiming, categorically, his right to the land.

--José Carlos Mariátegui

Purple Iris
08.01.2006
la regia cabeza, separada de tronco, permanecía intacta,
tal como si la hubieren acabado de cercenar,
y que de su sien derecha había nacido
un espléndido y fragante lirio
color violeta

quizá como símbolo de su regia estirpe,
o en señal inequívoco de glorificación de su holocausto

sacrificed by her dad

Dioses de Oaxaca

Stars in the rug represent the churches of Oaxaca
Why do I lie to myself?
Bluestones wet with rain
Fish,
embedded in the floor of the Abbaye de Lessay,
She agreed.
Xonaxi, Cosana
The rain, black spores.
Green stone arches and cupolas of blue and white squares
I will not publish this without your permission.
Violence, an aspect of love
Four points define
the corners of the universe.
Pije-tao, overlord of the 13 dieties
Strong-legged female statuettes
from San José Mogote

Street arts

Outsized puppets dance in Macedonia-Alcalá
Parental, pariente. Insistent, repetitive brass.
Confraternity band. Erratic counter-beat
Whisper of pantaloons
For a man to be a woman with a giant head
Scarf knotted under her chin.

Later in the callejón, interminable corridos of unrequited love.
Paired women dance the melody
Face-to-face, speaking heels, resonant on the tarima.

Share vials of mescal with new friends
Qué bueno, that lovers find one another tonight!
The children sleep on their mothers' laps.

Dust like pollen, green tint of limestone
Jade artifacts
Sacred to jaguar and serpent cults
Reason to dispense
with the opacities of writing
Hostage to Pedro Alvarado
the cacique bit off his own tongue

In the quiet of the Graphics Arts Institute Gallery
To study the nude self in charcoal
Turn away when the swan drinks her menstrual flow
Care in process imparts feeling to making
Replicas cut with less art, fantastic
In the pre-classical phase
Covarrubias noted evidence of mass manufacture,
a falling off in the quality of the cutting.

Bodies of evidence

Sopa de pez: peppery maximum, studying the light
Décor of Huatulco, sacked by Drake, 1578.
Across García Vigil, Trotsky's brain, exposed artifact
Centro Fotográfico Alvarez Bravo.
To document violence against workers,
corpse of a female tourist,
transvestites pose in a courtroom, expressive hand gestures.
Young violinists in pinstripes
(Casasola Family Archive).

What if one of the attendants stepped forward
with questions for me that I wanted to answer?
Thrust a knife into the table
Wooden tooth in the vein at the neck

Two women against a wall, photographed as if posing to be photographed, 1930.
A call to revolt. Cadaver in the alley his hat in place.
Murder of Mella, Tina Modotti, herself as herself,
staged to prove
innocence,
absolved, exposed.

The figure who looks at the stars: a figure within a figure,
father and son. Ribs irradiated,
rib cage of the god of death.
The figural sky of Rufino Tamayo,
History's component parts,
cut-away diagrams,
Skirt of astral transparency,
Francisco Gutiérrez.

A Nyarit man scratches his head, quizzical
Flat speckled stone
The hive in his stubby right hand
Universal womb

López-Carmona's studies in poly-angularity, applied to the construction of a school for the visual arts, joins expressionistic abstraction with purposeful design. Poly-angular studies on display in the Polanco home of David Alfaro Siqueiros figure primal exoticism and political commitment to a fully realized people's art in support of the popular front. Who defines the front if not the artist? who mourns?

Tinísima

Tina turned in her bed: those not aware of their freedom are not free. ... She felt violated by the judge's gaze. He looked like Ezra Pound, eyes like lakes or foxes. She pulled a thread out of her belly, from her breasts, she rose. Her skin hung over the rooftop wash line, from hook to hook. She wanted to climb down the iron stairs that the servants used. The fiery metal ate the raw flesh of her feet.

[after the text of Elena Poniatowska]

In the Jaguar's mouth

Ceremonial vessel, figural universe,
four points
define the maw of the cosmos.

Seated figures with children in their laps,
from the tombs of Edificio 1.

The dancers are men miming childbirth
They are slaves

At Dainzu, the ball game is visible
Ana Mendieta lay herself down
Mother to her child self
mimes rebirth
Silueta, from a tomb at Yagul

1973.

Visibility of power

The temple site
maps
the geography of the valley.
The *temascal* (steam lodge) faces west
Social tiers, reflected in construction and use of platforms
The year has 260 days
A pregnancy
The light
enters the tunnel
once each earthly cycle
The shaft at a right angle
Lay me down with wild chevril
Ipomoea turns the mountain white
Nopal, source of red dye

Téquio
Voluntary labor for the good of the community is
The ancients are closer to the gods

Today many from among the people are carpenters
From works comes prestige, gozoma

Many yet deny their heritage, betrayal,
My great Aunt, less forthcoming than her mother had been
Eyes that don't see, unfeeling heart

A salt from wood ash supplements diet,
nixtamalización

Few animal sources of protein, then
Guajolote
Equally

el macho es fácilmente identificable por sus actividades de pavoneo y gorgoreo.

In other words: to strut

Gansito, yummy chocolate-covered cake produced by the Marinela factory since 1956, the first snack cake of its kind in Latin America and a favorite of adults and kids alike! Copyright Bimbo Bakeries USA 2005 | All Rights Reserved

Another transcultural scenario, especially intended for children, for absolution is possible even after raiding the grocery store for maraschino cherries and candy bars, shared with other boys behind the vestry of St. Patrick's. The Blessed Virgin, Mother Goddess, is la diosa Tonantzín, she who is Coatlicue, la de la falda de serpientes, and bulls as in Crete of the Snake goddess, mounted bareback circus dancer, for sacrifice, black bulls of the best.

From within maternal caves
The baby's features were those of an embryonic jaguar.

San Agustín

From her garden
Jacarandas and calla lilies, azucena
I look down into the terraces of Monte Albán
Westerly
Haze
Burning dollop of sun
On this hillside
was a shirt factory, a clinic for the workers
An artisanal highschool.
The visibility of power,
stemming from blood lore,
fades
Census:
sixty six
Mixtec, Zapotec
New studios make
acid-free paper for kites and books
Régimen: usos y costumbres
A contract determines
the tariff structure
that propels
taxies from Etla
into Oaxaca. Travel permitted.
Llévame, llévame, carry me, carry me away
The carousel has broken down
Three little girls have no where to go
Barricades and conflagrations
A shot rips a shoulder.
The conflict hurts to the very bone
How govern
unless
each vote
counts.

Your desire for law and order
compromises your poetics.

Proud women

La Señora de Soledad
tiene una cara alba
On her altar of gold,
in her gown of gold
Black and white medallions
of her beneficence.
In her house, her son
hangs, dependent from
a vault of coiled gold.

Hyperbole of the cipher
Mayaguel is
The finery of goddesses
an infinity of beings
Torrential rain
softens clay
With four teats
Mother and virgin
Mixtec dress,
basket weavers,
red with gold bars
walking beside the road
toward the cattle pen.

Underlying expressions
are deeply erotic
transforms
Flowers for Angela
Polyangular
Singularly purposive
public insurrections
Badly educated
today's children want
to think for themselves
Reform travels
from Nochixtlán,
escuela primaria,
in waves that fall away
shy of the plunge
Terrorized
Always a mouth to feed

Talavera, maiolica

From tin-glazed earthenware
in the Spanish Baroque room,
learn that "cuencas" or "depressions"
produce effects that are to be
distinguished from
the "cuerda seca"
technique of al andalus. The cords,
coated with manganese
impregnated grease separate
isolate glazes. Wooden lattices
frame ceiling tiles.

How is it then that two pieces of Talavera
mean so much to some,
airport acquisitions, wall mounted
in my travel cupboard.
Interlaced, eightpoint, rose petal motif over white enamel,
could be Lindisfarne, absent the apocalyptical beasts.
Bright indigo with apple green motes of pollen,
pomegranate seeds
from Tangiers.
On a day of saturated tones,
holds sliced oranges.

Gigantesque

Backside of a naked man, Goya or Lucien Freud.
On a rural note, the green stripe of a Concord River
in the plane of transcendent fact (Barnet Newman)
courses like Rueda's *Guadalquiver*
through a creamy linen field.
Lines. Absolute and vertical.
Thoreau and Garcia Lorca
struggling to read
an immanence
recorded in the fields,
in Arabic and Sanskrit.
Elizabeth Murray's *Terrifying Terrain*
ties itself into knots, roseate, with worm and snake squiggles,
appliqué to metal foil.
No sense of profile as in Chocorua
The face of god.

From Frida's Restaurant

a marriage,
staged in a Norman Gothic keep, posing for friends.
Are weddings still conducted in Tehuantepec costume such as Frida wears
            in Nikolas Muray's photograph for the *Socialist Worker* (1942)?
Inescapably, chopped syntax, marks composition
Circumspection, obscene speculation
Less flamboyant than others with whom my shadow walks.
Robert Rauschenberg's 'combines'
            display a tactile uneasiness common among one-eyed poets
A haptic sense for texture and perspective.
Artifacts assembled for a private museum, sacred souvenirs
A thing language that functions like pointing, like isolation,
elements underscored, elements with super-saturated fluorescent colors
The muscular back of Guercino's *Samson,* spring or spur to the theme gigantesque
The detail of parquet floors in Artemesia Gentileschi's *Esther before Ahaseurus,*
            like Rueda's rusted textures, awakens a raw, ocular granularity
Flat sheets of baroque light also define the dance spaces of Limón's *Pavane of the Moor,*
soon, she said, to be performed again in Bellas Artes.
Whispering elders
had prompted my sister persona
to associate Emily Dickinson with Jenny Gage
A rifle across her bare legs.
Two friends confide their doubts about relations with men.
I add, I have a daughter your age
To share what I have felt:
How the hops used in German beers
have imprinted my memory palette.
That Claude McKay was a houseboy once
in so provincial New Hampshire, unable to experience the lilac nights
because his employment (like theirs)
required other
Susana came before them veiled
Was it under a holm oak or a mastik tree, betrayed accused
She had no choice but to comply
Rudely forced!
What compels obedience?
To openly address a new distance between lovers
Uncanny grace to dine here with others who also have a need to sort different perspectives.

White room
I contemplate this generous space among arcades
Ceiling bowed by the light
As if paper
Weddings here and wedding banquets
have been held
The way out
is a passage through
similar rooms
Funerals
For the father killed as he worked
artfully
to disentangle a landmine
from a vine
They carried him across the river in the bottom of the boat,
in his shroud
Mourners under an umbrella.
Impassive
Maroon roses

Corrido

Pride of the people in their heroes
Mio campeador
Epical valor and wisdom, honored by all,
News of deaths in the desert
Advocate of open boundaries

Who remembers today
the slain professor Güitrón?
Or the teachers at Luis Vives,
poets who taught the lost boys
in the time of fascist victories?

Who took to the streets with banderas
when the police opened fire
at Tlatelolco.
Athletes and students
of practical arts, ceramics, textiles.
Mothers and children
Who took the unedited photographs
of the corpses and the wounded?

And again it is May Day
In Los Angeles, Chicago and Nashua
New Hampshire, donde vivo.
Chorus of car horns
in solidarity, a people united.

Coatzacoalcos

In the center of the village on a wide open space, is a barn-like, towerless, white church, with a separate thatched shed for the old bronze bells. Inside the church there are no benches, no pulpit, no confessional, only rows of gaily painted niches and vitrines along the walls, arranged as in a museum, with arches of colored paper and tinseled flowers, and containing awkward wooden statues of saints, garishly painted, with staring glass eyes, all alike in size, as if to establish their equality. ... Never was Catholicism more on the surface than in this church that breathes paganism, or rather the reabsorption of Christian ideas into Indian mentality.

Miguel Covarrubias. *Mexico South: The Isthmus of Tehuántepec.* NY: Knopf, 1946 (42).

Sacrament

Different sopranos for different Christs
Shifts in rhythm instead of harmony
mark transitions. Dance replaces arias.

Calatrava's webs carry people through
tents with profiles that sweep across the sky.
Dana Schutz's palette of magazine colors
Multicolored mourners surround a broken corpse
theater of dismemberment and irony
Flatness, carnival, and mockery

Chorales with percussion from multiple sources
Cada persona tiene su mundo
She explained to her friend
Invented allegories of deep suffering

Muxima, site of pilgrimage,
choruses from multiple nations
La pasión según San Marco
Seeing double philosophical trees
Bound torso, folded drapery
Coils merge Bernini with cartoons
Mother nurses infants sprung from trees

Betrayed in the jungles of Bolivia
Fragments of his dismembered corpse
Circulated among the people
Genocide, slavery, environmental degradation
produced by conquistadors

Sacred sap of invented trees,
milky rubber stuff
Seeking a modern function
Each has her own world she said
examining the skin for imperfections

Suspended-finale
I had written my nine-month pastoral reverie
I wrote, wanting to make amends for everything I had ever written:

Faces of the oppressed
become crowds
A machete scored with letters
A People United
See he moves moving along the wall
The shadow of his camera
A white shirt, the boys shout
Distant gunfire
Black smoke of burning tires
Only kids, running, throwing stones
Let me pass
Then the red truck backs,
bang against the gate
Shots follow
The camera spins crazily
The focus, granular from the first frame
And rests on the pavement
under the claw of death
An insupportable stench adheres to the walls
In the glare of tear gas
exhort
desired order
in the throes of what you and I feared
to have become
Disciplina, disculpame

For Brad Will

About the Author

Born in Nashua, NH, USA, July 7, 1944; attended University of New Hampshire, 1962-67; US Army, 1968-71; graduate school, University of Oregon, 1971-75 (Doctor of Arts, concentrations in Old and Middle English, Modern Literature); 1975-1985: teaching in St. Croix USVI, Cambridge, Lowell and Boston MA, Cranberry Isles ME; during this period founded O.ARS (1981).

First appointed Assistant Professor of Writing & Humanities, Daniel Webster College, 1984; appointed Associate Professor 1989, Professor 1993.

Literary and Scholarly Achievements:
Until 1995, Wellman directed O.ARS, a literary and cultural organization, publishing anthologies of poetry, visual poetry, experimental prose, and commentary. Each volume explores an aspect of postmodern poetics. From its inception O.ARS published works of experimental or sur-fiction, visual poetry and other forms of writing associated with the international avant-garde, as well as what has come now to be known as language-centered writing.

Wellman's poetry and criticism have appeared in a variety of venues. A selected poems, spanning twenty years work, appeared in 1995 under the title, *Fields*. Wellman has given conference papers and published criticism on key modernist figures such as Ezra Pound, William Carlos Williams, and Charles Olson. He has also written and published on contemporary world poetry, especially that employing hybrid forms. In both his poetry and prose, Wellman engages a field poetics, using tropes like margin, frame or overlay to explore the ways in which cross-cultural contact or liminality produce meaning. He has translated contemporary poetry from French, German and Spanish sources. Current translation projects include *Jardín cerrado* by Emilio Prados and three books by Antonio Gamoneda, 2006 winner of the Cervantes prize.

OTHER TITLES FROM AHADADA

Ahadada Books publishes poetry. Preserving the best of the small press tradition, we produce finely designed and crafted books in limited editions.

Bela Fawr's Cabaret (David Annwn)   978-0-9808873-2-7

Writes Gavin Selerie: "David Annwn's work drills deep into strata of myth and history,. exposing devices which resonate in new contexts. Faithful to the living moment, his poems dip, hover and dart through soundscapes rich with suggestion, rhythmically charged and etymologically playful. Formally adventurous and inviting disjunction, these texts retain a lyric coherence that powerfully renders layers of experience. The mode veers from jazzy to mystical, evoking in the reader both disturbance and content. *Bela Fawr's Cabaret* has this recognisable stamp: music and legend 'Knocked Abaht a Bit', mischievous humour yielding subtle insight."

Age of the Demon Tools (Mark Spitzer)   978-0-9808873-1-0

Writes Ed Sanders: "You have to slow down, and absorb calmly, the procession of gritty, pointillist gnarls of poesy that Mark Spitzer wittily weaves into his book. Just the title, *Age of the Demon Tools*, is so appropriate in this horrid age of inappropriate technology—you know, corruptly programmed voting machines, drones with missiles hovering above huts, and mind reading machines looming just a few years into the demon-tool future. When you do slow down, and tarry within Spitzer's neologism-packed litanies, you will find the footprints of bards such as Allen Ginsberg, whose tradition of embedding current events into the flow of poesy is one of the great beacons of the new century. This book is worth reading if only for the poem 'Unholy Millenial Litany' and its blastsome truths."

Sweet Potatoes (Lou Rowan)   978-0-9781414-5-5

Lou Rowan . . . is retired, in love and charged. He was raised by horse breeders and went to Harvard and thus possesses an outward polish. But he talks like a radical, his speech incongruous with his buttoned-down appearance. *Golden Handcuffs Review*, the local literary magazine that Rowan founded and edits, is much like the man himself: appealing and presentable on the outside, a bit wild and experimental at the core.

Deciduous Poems (David B. Axelrod)   978-0-9808873-0-3

Dr. David B. Axelrod has published hundreds of articles and poems as well as sixteen books of poetry. Among his many grants and awards, he is recipient of three Fulbright Awards including his being the first official Fulbright Poet-in-Residence in the People's Republic of China. He was featured in Newsday as a "Star in his academic galaxy," and characterized by the New York Times as "a treat." He has shared the stage with such notables as Louis Simpson, X. J. Kennedy, William Stafford, Robert Bly, Allen Ginsburg, David Ignatow and Galway Kinnell, in performance for the U.N., the American Library Association, the Struga Festival, and hundreds more schools and public events. His poetry has been translated into fourteen languages and he is a frequent and celebrated master teacher.

Late Poems of Lu You (Burton Watson)   978-0-9781414-9-3

Lu You (1125–1210) whose pen name was 'The Old Man Who Does as He Pleases,' was among the most prolific of Chinese poets, having left behind a collection of close to ten thousand poems as well as miscellaneous prose writings. His poetry, often characterized by an intense patriotism, is also notable for its recurrent expression of a carefree enjoyment of life. This volume consists of twenty-five of Burton Watson's new translations, plus Lu You's poems as they appear in the original, making this a perfect collection for the lay reader as well as for those with a mastery of Song dynasty Chinese.

www.ahadada.com

Oulipoems (Philip Terry)   978-0-978-1414-2-4

Philip Terry was born in Belfast in 1962 and has been working with Oulipian and related writing practices for over twenty years. His lipogrammatic novel *The Book of Bachelors* (1999), was highly praised by the Oulipo: "Enormous rigour, great virtuosity—but that's the least of it." Currently he is Director of Creative Writing at the University of Essex, where he teaches a graduate course on the poetics of constraint. His work has been published in *Panurge*, *PN Review*, *Oasis*, *North American Review* and *Onedit*, and his books include the celebrated anthology of short stories *Ovid Metamorphosed* (2000) and *Fables of Aesop* (2006). His translation of Raymond Queneau's last book of poems, *Elementary Morality*, is forthcoming from Carcanet. *Oulipoems* is his first book of poetry.

The Impossibility of Dreams (David Axelrod)   978-0-9781414-3-1

Writes Louis Simpson: "Whether Axelrod is reliving a moment of pleasure, or a time of bitterness and pain, the truth of his poetry is like life itself compelling." Dr. David B. Axelrod has published hundreds of articles and poems as well as sixteen books of poetry. Among his many grants and awards, he is recipient of three Fulbright Awards including his being the first official Fulbright Poet-in-Residence in the People's Republic of China . He was featured in *Newsday* as a "Star in his academic galaxy," and characterized by the *New York Times* as "A Treat." His poetry has been translated into fourteen languages and he is a frequent and celebrated master teacher.

Now Showing (Jim Daniels)   0-9781414-1-5

Of Jim Daniels, the *Harvard Review* writes, "Although Daniels' verse is thematically dark, the energy and beauty of his language and his often brilliant use of irony affirm that a lighter side exists. This poet has already found his voice. And he speaks with that rare urgency that demands we listen." This is affirmed by Carol Muske, who identifies the "melancholy sweetness" running through these poems that identifies him as "a poet born to praise".

China Notes & The Treasures of Dunhuang (Jerome Rothenberg)   0-9732233-9-1

"*The China Notes* come from a trip in 2002 that brought us out as far as the Gobi Desert & allowed me to see some of the changes & continuities throughout the country. I was traveling with poet & scholar Wai-lim Yip & had a chance to read poetry in five or six cities & to observe things as part of an ongoing discourse with Wai-lim & others. The ancient beauty of some of what we saw played out against the theme park quality of other simulacra of the past....A sense of beckoning wilderness/wildness in a landscape already cut into to serve the human need for power & control." So Jerome Rothenberg describes the events behind the poems in this small volume—a continuation of his lifelong exploration of poetry and the search for a language to invoke the newness and strangeness both of what we observe and what we can imagine.

The Passion of Phineas Gage & Selected Poems (Jesse Glass)   0-9732233-8-3

The Passion of Phineas Gage & Selected Poems presents the best of Glass' experimental writing in a single volume. Glass' ground-breaking work has been hailed by poets as diverse as Jerome Rothenberg, William Bronk and Jim Daniels for its insight into human nature and its exploration of forms. Glass uses the tools of postmodernism: collaging, fragmentation, and Oulipo-like processes along with a keen understanding of poetic forms and traditions that stretches back to Beowulf and beyond. Moreover, Glass finds his subject matter in larger-than-life figures like Phineas Gage—the man whose life was changed in an instant when an iron bar was sent rocketing through his brain in a freak accident—as well as in ants processing up a wall in time to harpsichord music in order to steal salt crystals from the inner lip of a cowrie shell. The range and ambition of his work sets it apart. The product of over 30 years of engagement with the avant-garde, *The Passion of Phineas Gage & Selected Poems* is the work of a mature poet who continues to reinvent himself with every text he produces.

www.ahadada.com

*aha***dada**

b o o k s

Send a request to be added to our mailing list:
http://www.ahadadabooks.com/

Ahadada Books are available from these fine distributors:

Canada
Ahadada Books
3158 Bentworth Drive
Burlington, Ontario
Canada, L7M 1M2
Phone: (905) 617-7754
http://www.ahadadabooks.com

United States of America
Small Press Distribution
1341 Seventh Street
Berkeley, CA 94710-1409
Phone: (510) 524-1668
Fax: (510) 524-0852
http://www.spdbooks.org/

Europe
West House Books
40 Crescent Road
Nether Edge, Sheffield
United Kingdom S7 1HN
Phone: 0114-2586035
http://www.westhousebooks.co.uk/

Japan
Intercontinental Marketing Corp.
Centre Building 2nd floor
1-14-13 Iriya, Taitoku
Tokyo 110-0013
Telephone 81-3-3876-3073
http://www.imcbook.net/